Reteach Book

Grade 2

PROVIDES Tier 1 Intervention for Every Lesson

HOUGHTON MIFFLIN HARCOURT

Printed in the U.S.A.

ISBN 978-0-547-39280-6

     5 6 7 8 9 10 0982 15 14 13 12 11

4500333127   ^ B C D E F G

Contents

BIG IDEA 1: Number and Place Value

Chapter 1: Number Concepts

Chapter 2: Numbers to 1,000

BIG IDEA 2: Addition, Subtraction, Multiplication, and Data

Chapter 3: Basic Facts and Relationships

Chapter 4: 2-Digit Addition

Chapter 5: 2-Digit Subtraction

Chapter 6: Data

Chapter 7: 3-Digit Addition and Subtraction

Chapter 8: Multiplication Concepts

BIG IDEA 3: Measurement and Geometry

Chapter 9: Length

Chapter 10: Weight, Mass, and Capacity

Chapter 11: Money and Time

Chapter 12: Geometry and Patterns

Understand Place Value

0, 1, 2, 3, 4, 5, 6, 7, 8, and 9 are **digits**.
You can tell the value of a digit by
looking at its place in the number.

When you write 52,
you use two digits.

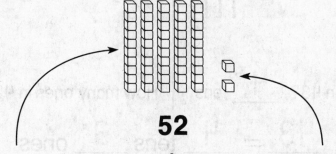

52

The digit __5__ is in the tens place.

It tells you that 52 has __5__ tens.

Its value is __50__.

The digit __2__ is in the ones place.

It tells you that 52 has __2__ ones.

Its value is __2__.

Circle the value of the underlined digit.

1. 27

    20   2

2. 18

    1   10

3. 56

    60   6

4. 30

    30   3

5. 75
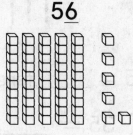

    5   50

6. 41
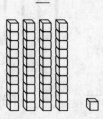

    4   40

Expanded Form

You can describe the number 43 in different ways.

Tens	Ones

How many tens in 43? __4__ tens | How many ones in 43? __3__ ones

$$\underline{43} = \underline{4} \text{ tens } \underline{3} \text{ ones}$$

$$\underline{43} = \underline{40} + \underline{3}$$

Describe the number in two ways.

1. 35

35 = _____ tens _____ ones

35 = _____ + _____

2. 63

63 = _____ tens _____ ones

63 = _____ + _____

3. 57

57 = _____ tens _____ ones

57 = _____ + _____

4. 19

19 = _____ ten _____ ones

19 = _____ + _____

Different Ways to Write Numbers

You can write numbers in different ways.

$$20 + 6$$

____2____ tens ____6____ ones

twenty-six

26

ones	teen words		tens	
I one	II eleven	I ten I one	I0 ten	I ten
2 two	I2 twelve	I ten 2 ones	20 twenty	2 tens
3 three	I3 thirteen	I ten 3 ones	30 thirty	3 tens
4 four	I4 fourteen	I ten 4 ones	40 forty	4 tens
5 five	I5 fifteen	I ten 5 ones	50 fifty	5 tens
6 six	I6 sixteen	I ten 6 ones	60 sixty	6 tens
7 seven	I7 seventeen	I ten 7 ones	70 seventy	7 tens
8 eight	I8 eighteen	I ten 8 ones	80 eighty	8 tens
9 nine	I9 nineteen	I ten 9 ones	90 ninety	9 tens

Write the number another way.

I. twenty

_____

2. 37

_____ tens _____ ones

3. 40 + 5

_____

4. eighty-one

_____

5. 56

_____

6. 9 tens 2 ones

_____

7. I ten 8 ones

_____

8. seventy-three

_____ tens _____ ones

Different Names for Numbers

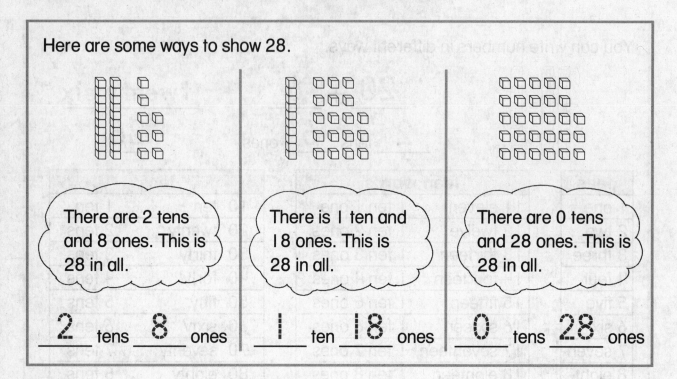

Here are some ways to show 28.

There are 2 tens and 8 ones. This is 28 in all.

There is 1 ten and 18 ones. This is 28 in all.

There are 0 tens and 28 ones. This is 28 in all.

__2__ tens __8__ ones

__1__ ten __18__ ones

__0__ tens __28__ ones

Write how many tens and ones.

1. 32

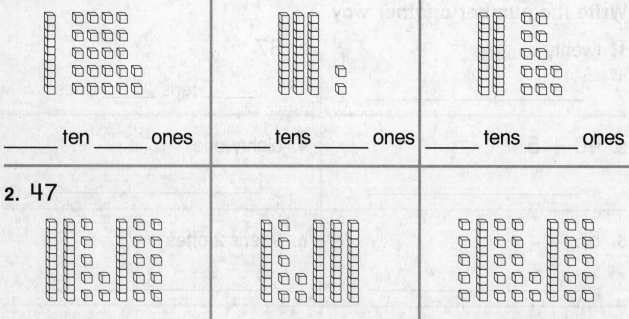

_____ ten _____ ones

_____ tens _____ ones

_____ tens _____ ones

2. 47

_____ tens _____ ones

_____ tens _____ ones

_____ tens _____ ones

Problem Solving
Make a List • Tens and Ones

Anya is sorting 25 toys. She can sort them into groups of 10 toys or as single toys. What are the different ways Anya can sort the toys?

Unlock the Problem

What do I need to find?

the different ways

Anya can sort the toys

What information do I need to use?

She can sort them into

groups of 10 toys or as

single toys.

Show how to solve the problem.

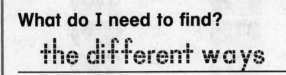 2 tens + 5 ones

1 ten + 15 ones

0 tens + 25 ones

Groups of 10 toys	Single toys
2	5
1	15

Make a list to solve.

1. Mr. Moore is buying 29 apples. He can buy them in packs of 10 apples or as single apples. What are the different ways Mr. Moore can buy the apples?

Packs of 10 apples	Single apples
2	
1	
0	

Even and Odd Numbers

These are even numbers.
They are shown with pairs with no cubes left over.

4 is even.   6 is even.   8 is even.   10 is even.

These are odd numbers.
They are shown with pairs with 1 cube left over.

3 is odd.   5 is odd.   7 is odd.   9 is odd.

Count out the number of cubes.
Make pairs. Then write **even** or **odd**.

1. 15 _____	**2.** 11 _____
3. 12 _____	**4.** 13 _____
5. 16 _____	**6.** 14 _____

Algebra: Compare and Order Numbers to 100

You can compare models to
help you compare numbers.

38 $\bigcirc>$ 33

38 is greater than 33.

3 tens = 3 tens
The tens are the same, so I
need to compare the ones.

8 ones > 3 ones

So, 38 > 33.

Compare the numbers. Write >, <, or =.

1.   32 $\bigcirc$ 42

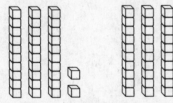

2.   18 $\bigcirc$ 13

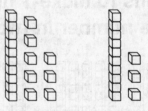

3.   46 $\bigcirc$ 38

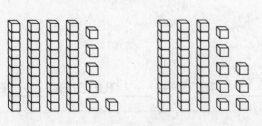

4.   24 $\bigcirc$ 24

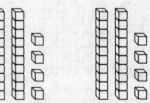
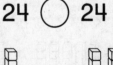

Hundreds

There are 10 tens in 1 hundred.

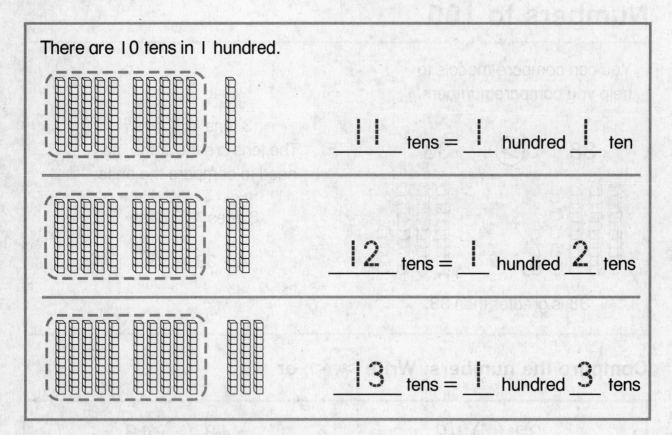

_11_ tens = _1_ hundred _1_ ten

_12_ tens = _1_ hundred _2_ tens

_13_ tens = _1_ hundred _3_ tens

Circle tens to make 1 hundred.
Write the number in two ways.

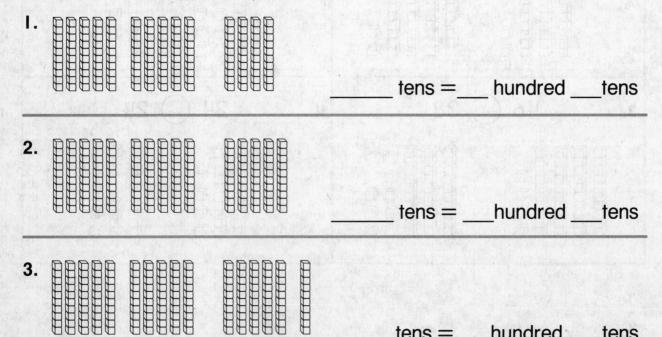

1. _____ tens = ___ hundred ___ tens

2. _____ tens = ___ hundred ___ tens

3. _____ tens = ___ hundred ___ tens

Model 3-Digit Numbers

You can use blocks to show 243.

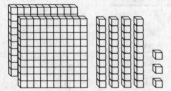

Hundreds	Tens	Ones
2	4	3

The number 243 has
2 hundreds, 4 tens, and
3 ones.

Write how many hundreds, tens, and ones.

1.

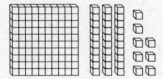

Hundreds	Tens	Ones

2.

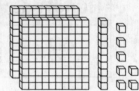

Hundreds	Tens	Ones

3.

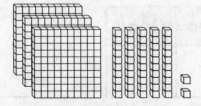

Hundreds	Tens	Ones

4.

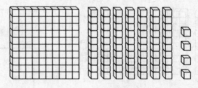

Hundreds	Tens	Ones

Hundreds, Tens, and Ones

How many are there in all?

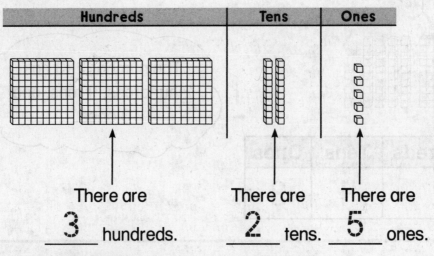

Hundreds	Tens	Ones

There are _3_ hundreds. There are _2_ tens. _5_ ones.

Write how many in the chart.

Hundreds	Tens	Ones
3	2	5

3 hundreds 2 tens 5 ones is the same as __325__.

Write how many hundreds, tens, and ones. Write the number.

1.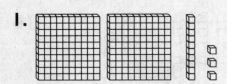

Hundreds	Tens	Ones

_____

2.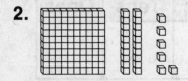

Hundreds	Tens	Ones

_____

Place Value to 1,000

You know the value of each digit in 426
by its place in the number.

Hundreds	Tens	Ones

The digit 4 tells you there are 4 hundreds. Its value is **400**.

The digit 2 tells you there are 2 tens. Its value is **20**.

The digit 6 tells you there are 6 ones. Its value is **6**.

Circle the value or the meaning of the underlined digit.

1. 7<u>8</u>2	800	80	8
2. <u>3</u>52	3 hundreds	3 tens	3
3. 7<u>4</u>2	4	40	400
4. 41<u>9</u>	9 hundreds	9 tens	9 ones
5. <u>5</u>84	500	50	5

Name _____

Different Forms of Numbers

There is more than one way to write a number.

three hundred sixty-two

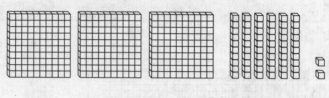

__3__ hundreds __6__ tens __2__ ones

__300__ + __60__ + __2__

__362__

Write the number in different ways.

1.    four hundred thirty-two

_____ hundreds _____ tens _____ ones

_____ + _____ + _____

_____

2. 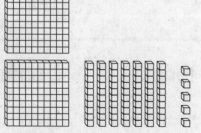   two hundred seventy-five

_____ hundreds _____ tens _____ ones

_____ + _____ + _____

_____

Different Ways to Show Numbers

These two models can both be used
to show the number 324.

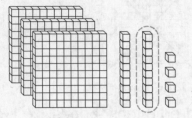

Hundreds	Tens	Ones
3	2	4

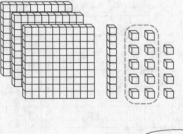

Hundreds	Tens	Ones
3	1	14

10 ones have the
same value as 1 ten.

Write how many hundreds, tens, and ones.

1. 132

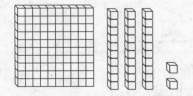

Hundreds	Tens	Ones

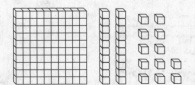

Hundreds	Tens	Ones

Name _____

Count by 10s and 100s

10 less and 10 more	100 less and 100 more

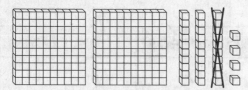

10 less than 234 is
2 hundreds 2 tens 4 ones.

224

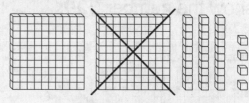

100 less than 234 is
1 hundred 3 tens 4 ones.

134

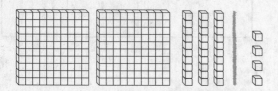

10 more than 234 is
2 hundreds 4 tens 4 ones.

244

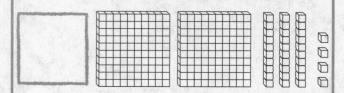

100 more than 234 is
3 hundreds 3 tens 4 ones.

334

Write the number.

1. 10 more than 719

   _____

2. 10 less than 246

   _____

3. 100 more than 291

   _____

4. 100 less than 687

   _____

5. 10 less than 568

   _____

6. 100 more than 649

   _____

Algebra: Number Patterns

Compare the digits in each place to find a pattern.

421, 431, 441, 451, ⬛, ⬛

Which digits change from
number to number?

The __tens__ digits change.

How do these digits change?

by __one__ each time

The numbers from the pattern are
shaded on the chart. Skip count to find
the next two numbers in the pattern.

401	402	403	404	405	406	407	408	409	410
411	412	413	414	415	416	417	418	419	420
421	422	423	424	425	426	427	428	429	430
431	432	433	434	435	436	437	438	439	440
441	442	443	444	445	446	447	448	449	450
451	452	453	454	455	456	457	458	459	460
461	462	463	464	465	466	467	468	469	470
471	472	473	474	475	476	477	478	479	480
481	482	483	484	485	486	487	488	489	490
491	492	493	494	495	496	497	498	499	500

The next two numbers are __461__ and __471__.

**Compare the digits in each place to
find the next two numbers.**

1. 937, 947, 957, 967, ⬛, ⬛

   The next two numbers are _____ and _____.

2. 135, 235, 335, 435, ⬛, ⬛

   The next two numbers are _____ and _____.

Problem Solving

Make a Model • Compare Numbers

At the zoo, there are 137 birds and 142 reptiles.

Are there more birds or more reptiles at the zoo?

Unlock the Problem

What do I need to find?	**What information do I need to use?**
I need to find if there are more __birds__ or __reptiles__ .	There are __137__ birds. There are __142__ reptiles.

Show how to solve the problem.

Draw quick pictures to use as a model.

Birds

Reptiles

Compare the hundreds first. Then compare the tens if you need to.

There are more _____ at the zoo.

Draw quick pictures to use as a model.

1. There are 153 birds and 149 fish at the nature center.
   Are there more birds or more fish?

There are more _____ at the nature center.

Name _____

Algebra: Compare Numbers

You can compare 3-digit numbers.
First, compare the hundreds.

213 $>$ 113

213 has more hundreds
than 113.
213 is greater than 113.

If the hundreds are the same, compare the tens.

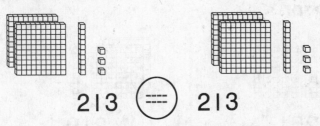

213 $<$ 243

213 has fewer tens
than 243.
213 is less than 243.

If the hundreds and tens are the same,
compare the ones.

213 $=$ 213

They have the same
number of hundreds, tens,
and ones.
213 is equal to 213.

Write **is greater than**, **is less than**, or **is equal to**.
Then write $>$, $<$, or $=$.

1.

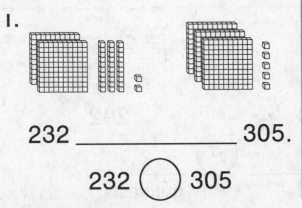

232 _____ 305.

232 ◯ 305

2.

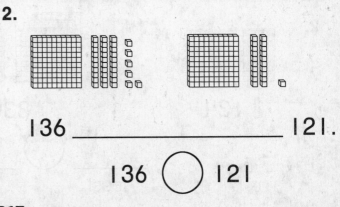

136 _____ 121.

136 ◯ 121

Algebra: Order Numbers

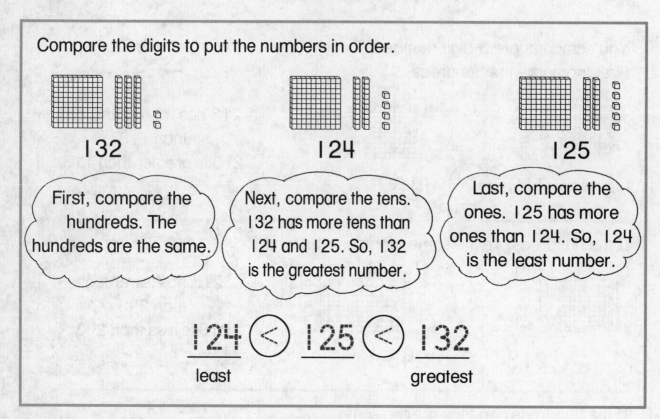

Compare the digits to put the numbers in order.

132   124   125

First, compare the hundreds. The hundreds are the same.

Next, compare the tens. 132 has more tens than 124 and 125. So, 132 is the greatest number.

Last, compare the ones. 125 has more ones than 124. So, 124 is the least number.

124 $<$ 125 $<$ 132

least   greatest

Compare the numbers. Write them in order from least to greatest. Then write $>$ or $<$.

1.

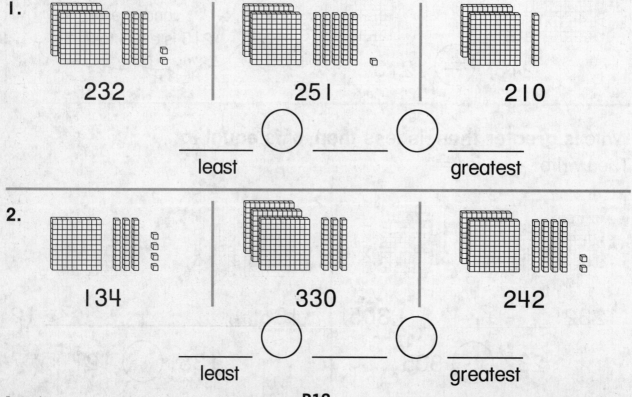

232   251   210

_____ ⃝ _____ ⃝ _____
least   greatest

2.

134   330   242

_____ ⃝ _____ ⃝ _____
least   greatest

Addition Facts

Use what you already know to help you find sums.

If you know $4 + 4$,
you can solve $4 + 5$.

☆☆☆☆ ★★★★
$4 + 4 = \underline{8}$

Because 5 is I more than 4,
$4 + 5$ is I more than $4 + 4$.

☆☆☆☆ ★★★★★
$4 + 5 = \underline{9}$

You can add in any order.

☆☆☆ ★★★★★
$3 + 5 = \underline{8}$

If you know $3 + 5$,
then you know $5 + 3$.

★★★★★ ☆☆☆
$5 + 3 = \underline{8}$

If you add zero to any number,
the sum is that number.

☆☆☆☆☆
$5 + 0 = \underline{5}$

Write the sums.

1. $5 + 7 = \underline{12}$

   $7 + 5 = \underline{12}$

2. $\underline{} = 9 + 6$

   $\underline{} = 6 + 9$

3. $6 + 0 = \underline{}$

   $8 + 0 = \underline{}$

4. $\underline{} = 9 + 5$

   $\underline{} = 5 + 9$

5. $7 + 7 = \underline{}$

   $7 + 8 = \underline{}$

6. $9 + 2 = \underline{}$

   $2 + 9 = \underline{}$

7. $\underline{} = 3 + 6$

   $\underline{} = 6 + 3$

8. $4 + 0 = \underline{}$

   $5 + 0 = \underline{}$

9. $8 + 8 = \underline{}$

   $8 + 9 = \underline{}$

Make-a-Ten Facts

You can make a ten to find sums.

$8 + 5 =$ ___?___ .

Step ❶ Start with the greater addend.
Break apart the other addend to make a ten.

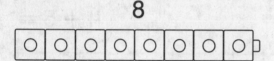   +   

You need to add **2** to 8 to make a ten.
So, break apart 5 as **2** and 3.

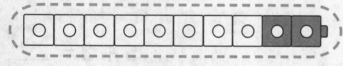

$8 + 2 = 10$ 3

Step ❷ Add on the rest to the 10.

> **Think:** I added 2 to make a ten.
> Then I add the 3 I have left.

$10 +$ __3__ $=$ __13__

Step ❸ Write the sum. $8 + 5 =$ __13__

Write the sum. Show the make-a-ten fact you used.

1. $7 + 6 =$ ___	2. $9 + 2 =$ ___	3. $4 + 8 =$ ___
$10 +$ ___ $=$ ___	$10 +$ ___ $=$ ___	$10 +$ ___ $=$ ___
4. $5 + 9 =$ ___	5. $8 + 6 =$ ___	6. $4 + 9 =$ ___
$10 +$ ___ $=$ ___	$10 +$ ___ $=$ ___	$10 +$ ___ $=$ ___

Add 3 Addends

Remember: Changing the way numbers are grouped does not change the sum.

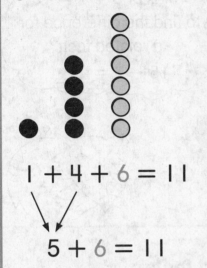

$1 + 4 + 6 = 11$

$5 + 6 = 11$

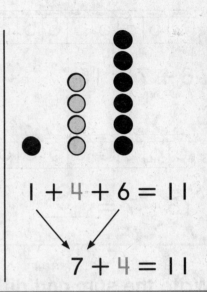

$1 + 4 + 6 = 11$

$1 + 10 = 11$

$1 + 4 + 6 = 11$

$7 + 4 = 11$

Solve two ways. Circle the two addends you add first.

1. $5 + 3 + 5 = $ ____ $5 + 3 + 5 = $ ____

2. $7 + 2 + 3 = $ ____ $7 + 2 + 3 = $ ____

3. $1 + 1 + 9 = $ ____ $1 + 1 + 9 = $ ____

4. $6 + 4 + 4 = $ ____ $6 + 4 + 4 = $ ____

Name _____

Relate Addition and Subtraction

Use addition facts to help you subtract.

$8 + 7 = 15$

Think of $8 + 7 = 15$ to find the difference for a related fact:

$15 - 7 = $ ___ .

$15 - 7 = \underline{8}$

Write the sum and difference for the related facts.

1. $8 + 9 = \underline{17}$

   $17 - 9 = \underline{8}$

2. $7 + 6 = $ ___

   $13 - 7 = $ ___

3. $6 + 8 = $ ___

   $14 - 8 = $ ___

4. $9 + 9 = $ ___

   $18 - 9 = $ ___

5. $8 + 4 = $ ___

   $12 - 4 = $ ___

6. $8 + 8 = $ ___

   $16 - 8 = $ ___

7. $9 + 7 = $ ___

   $16 - 7 = $ ___

8. $7 + 5 = $ ___

   $12 - 7 = $ ___

Name _____

Fact Families

In a fact family you use the same numbers in addition and subtraction facts. You can make a fact family with the numbers **3**, **6**, and **9**.

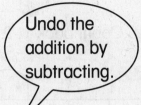

Undo the addition by subtracting.

$3 + 6 = \underline{9}$ $\qquad$ $9 - 3 = \underline{6}$

$\underline{6} + \underline{3} = \underline{9}$ $\qquad$ $\underline{9} - \underline{6} = \underline{3}$

Complete the fact family.

1. (6 / 1 5)

$1 + 5 = \underline{}$ $\qquad$ $6 - 5 = \underline{}$

$\underline{} + \underline{} = \underline{}$ $\qquad$ $\underline{} - \underline{} = \underline{}$

2. (8 / 0 8)

$8 + 0 = \underline{}$ $\qquad$ $8 - \underline{} = 8$

$\underline{} + \underline{} = \underline{}$ $\qquad$ $\underline{} - \underline{} = \underline{}$

3. (11 / 7 4)

$7 + 4 = \underline{}$ $\qquad$ $11 - \underline{} = 7$

$\underline{} + \underline{} = \underline{}$ $\qquad$ $\underline{} - \underline{} = \underline{}$

4. (12 / 9 3)

$9 + 3 = \underline{}$ $\qquad$ $12 - 3 = \underline{}$

$\underline{} + \underline{} = \underline{}$ $\qquad$ $\underline{} - \underline{} = \underline{}$

Name _____

Subtraction Facts

These are some ways to remember differences.

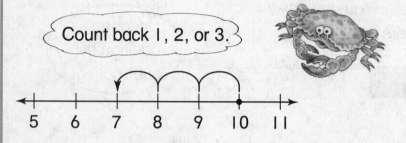

Count back 1, 2, or 3.

5 6 7 8 9 10 11

$10 - 1 = \underline{9}$

$10 - 2 = \underline{8}$

$10 - 3 = \underline{7}$

Think addition to subtract.

$6 + 4 = \underline{10}$

so, $10 - 4 = \underline{6}$

Think of subtraction facts in a fact family.

$9 + 4 = \underline{13}$ $13 - 9 = \underline{4}$

$4 + 9 = \underline{13}$ $13 - 4 = \underline{9}$

Write the difference.

1. $13 - 5 = \underline{8}$

2. $15 - 8 = \underline{}$

3. $12 - 3 = \underline{}$

4. $11 - 2 = \underline{}$

5. $9 - 3 = \underline{}$

6. $12 - 5 = \underline{}$

7. $16 - 8 = \underline{}$

8. $13 - 7 = \underline{}$

9. $10 - 4 = \underline{}$

10. $14 - 7 = \underline{}$

Represent Addition and Subtraction

There are 5 girls and 11 boys at the park.
How many more boys than girls are at the park?

You can use bar models to help you add or subtract.

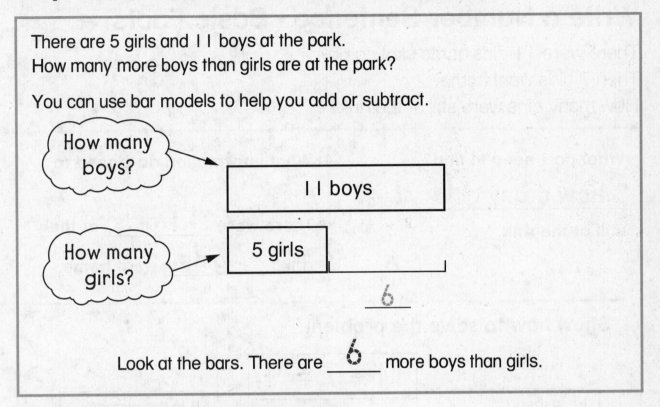

How many boys?

11 boys

How many girls?

5 girls

6

Look at the bars. There are ___6___ more boys than girls.

Complete the bar model to solve.

1. Nathan had 7 stamps. Then he got 9 more stamps.
   How many stamps does Nathan have in all?

7 stamps	9 stamps

_____ stamps in all

_____ stamps

2. Jeni had 13 pennies. She gave 5 pennies to
   Amy. How many pennies does Jeni have left?

gave 5 pennies	_____ pennies left

13 pennies

_____ pennies

Problem Solving
Write a Number Sentence • Basic Facts

There were 11 girls at the skating rink.
Then 7 girls went home.
How many girls were still at the rink?

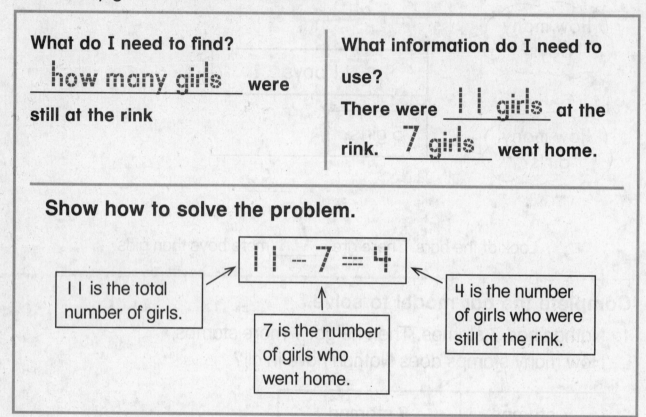

What do I need to find?

how many girls were
still at the rink

What information do I need to use?

There were 11 girls at the
rink. 7 girls went home.

Show how to solve the problem.

$$11 - 7 = 4$$

11 is the total number of girls.

7 is the number of girls who went home.

4 is the number of girls who were still at the rink.

Write a number sentence to solve the problem.

1. Elizabeth has 4 books about trees and 5 books about flowers. How many books about trees or flowers does she have?

___ ◯ ___ ◯ ___

_____ books

2. There were 16 children playing kickball. Some went home. Then there were 8 children playing kickball. How many children went home?

___ ◯ ___ ◯ ___

_____ children

Name _____

Algebra: Balance Number Sentences

What number will complete the number sentence?

$$8 + 1 = 2 + \boxed{}$$

$$9 = 2 + \boxed{}$$

So, $8 + 1 = 2 + \boxed{7}$.

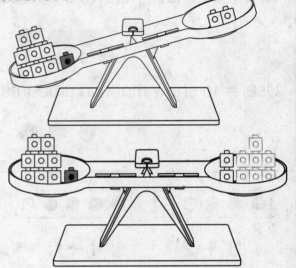

Write the number that will complete the number sentence.

1. $5 + 7 = 8 +$ ____

    12

2. $5 + 4 = 7 +$ ____

3. $6 + 2 = 3 +$ ____

4. $3 + 4 = 2 +$ ____

5. $3 + 8 = 7 +$ ____

6. $6 + 4 = 3 +$ ____

Equal and Not Equal

Use = to show that two amounts are equal.

● ● ● = ● ● ●

Use ≠ to show that two amounts are not equal.

● ● ● ≠ ● ● ● ●

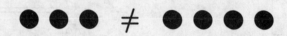

3 + 2   4 + 1

5 = 5

So, 3 + 2 ⟨=⟩ 4 + 1.

3 + 1   1 + 2

4 ≠ 3

So, 3 + 1 ⟨≠⟩ 1 + 2.

Write = or ≠ to make the number sentence true.

1. 4 + 4 ◯ 7 + 1

2. 8 + 0 ◯ 3 + 6

3. 8 − 5 ◯ 14 − 7

4. 15 − 8 ◯ 12 − 5

5. 7 + 2 ◯ 13 − 4

6. 12 − 4 ◯ 6 + 2

Break Apart Ones to Add

Sometimes when you are adding, you can break apart ones to make a ten.

$37 + 8 = $ __?__

Look at the two-digit addend, 37. What digit

is in the ones place? __7__

Decide how many you need to add to the ones digit to make 10.

$7 + $ __3__ $ = 10$, and $37 + $ __3__ $ = 40$

Take away that number from the one-digit addend, 8.

$8 - 3 = 5$

Finally, write the new number sentence. $40 + 5 = $ __45__

Find the sum. Write or draw to show what you did.

1. $28 + 6 = $ ___

2. $34 + 7 = $ ___

Name _____

Use Compensation

This is a way to add 2-digit numbers.
Take ones from one addend to make the other addend a ten.

$27 + 38 = \underline{\ ?\ }$

First, find the addend with the greater ones digit. $\underline{38}$
How many ones would you need to add to make it a tens number?

$38 + \underline{\ \ \ } = 40$ Add $\underline{\ 2\ }$ to make $\underline{40}$.

Next, take that many ones away from the other addend.

$27 - 2 = 25$ The two new addends are $\underline{25}$ and $\underline{40}$.

Write the new addition sentence to find the sum.

$\underline{25} + \underline{40} = \underline{65}$

Show how to make one addend a tens number. Complete the new addition sentence.

1. $28 + 16 = ?$

$\underline{\ \ \ } + \underline{\ \ \ } = \underline{\ \ \ }$

2. $37 + 24 = ?$

$\underline{\ \ \ } + \underline{\ \ \ } = \underline{\ \ \ }$

Break Apart Addends
as Tens and Ones

25 + 46 = ?

Break apart 25 into tens and ones.   Break apart 46 into tens and ones.

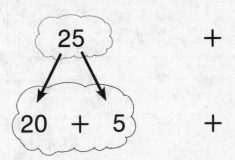   +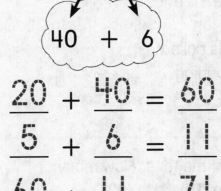

Then, add the tens from the two addends.

$$\underline{20} + \underline{40} = \underline{60}$$

Add the ones from the two addends.

$$\underline{5} + \underline{6} = \underline{11}$$

Add the two sums.

$$\underline{60} + \underline{11} = \underline{71}$$

So, 25 + 46 = $\underline{71}$.

Break apart the addends. Solve for the total sum.

1.   12   +   48 = ?

___ + ___ + ___ + ___

Add the tens.   ___ + ___ = ___

Add the ones.   ___ + ___ = ___

How many in all?   ___ + ___ = ___

So, 12 + 48 = ___.

Model Regrouping for Addition

Add 18 and 25.
Show 18 and 25 with ▭▭▭▭▭▭ ▫.
Count the ones.
How many ones are there in all? __13__ ones

Can you make a ten? __yes__

Tens	Ones

Trade 10 ones
for 1 ten.
This is called
regrouping.

Tens	Ones

Count the tens. How many
tens are there in all? __4__ tens

Count the ones. How many
ones are there in all? __3__ ones

__4__ tens __3__ ones is the same as __43__.

Tens	Ones

Write how many tens and ones in the sum.
Write the sum.

1. Add 46 and 19.

Tens	Ones

____ tens ____ ones

____

2. Add 45 and 27.

Tens	Ones

____ tens ____ ones

____

3. Add 58 and 38.

Tens	Ones

____ tens ____ ones

____

Model and Record 2-Digit Addition

Model 33 + 19.

How many ones are there in all? __12__ ones

Can you make a ten? __yes__

Tens	Ones
□	
3	3
+ 1	9

Regroup 10 ones as 1 ten.
Write a 1 in the tens column
to show the regrouped ten.

How many ones are left
after regrouping? __2__ ones

Write that number in the ones place.

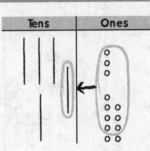

Tens	Ones
▫	
3	3
+ 1	9
	2

How many tens
are there in all? __5__ tens

Write that number
in the tens place.

Tens	Ones
1	
3	3
+ 1	9
5	2

Draw quick pictures for the problem. Write the sum.

1.
Tens	Ones
□	
4	7
+ 2	5

Tens	Ones

2.
Tens	Ones
□	
3	6
+ 4	6

Tens	Ones

2-Digit Addition

Add 27 and 36.

STEP 1	STEP 2	STEP 3
Model 27 and 36. Add the ones. $7 + 6 = 13$	If you can make a 10, regroup 10 ones for 1 ten. $13 \text{ ones} = 1 \text{ ten } 3 \text{ ones}$	Add the tens. Remember to add the regrouped ten. $1 + 2 + 3 = 6$

STEP 1

Tens	Ones
	2 7
+	3 6

STEP 2

Tens	Ones
	2 7
+	3 6
	3

STEP 3

Tens	Ones
1	2 7
+	3 6
6	3

Regroup if you need to. Write the sum.

1.

Tens	Ones
	5 4
+	2 9

2.

Tens	Ones
	1 7
+	6 1

3.

Tens	Ones
	4 1
+	2 9

4.

Tens	Ones
	3 5
+	3 2

Practice 2-Digit Addition

Eliza sold 47 pencils in one week.
She sold 35 pencils the next week.
How many pencils did she sell in all?

Add 47 and 35. Add the ones. $7 + 5 = 12$	Regroup. 12 ones = 1 ten and 2 ones	Add the tens. $1 + 4 + 3 = 8$

□
  4 | 7
+ 3 | 5
	1
	  4 | 7
	+ 3 | 5
	    | 2
		1
		  4 | 7
		+ 3 | 5
		  8 | 2

Write the sum.

1. □
  4 | 3
+ 1 | 9

2. □
  5 | 6
+ 1 | 8

3. □
  3 | 8
+ 4 | 2

4. □
  2 | 3
+ 4 | 5

5. □
  1 | 2
+ 4 | 9

6. □
  8 | 1
+ 1 | 7

7. □
  2 | 9
+ 4 | 7

8. □
  5 | 1
+ 3 | 8

Rewrite 2-Digit Addition

Add. $43 + 19 = ?$

STEP 1	STEP 2	STEP 3
What is the tens digit in 43? __4__ Write 4 in the tens column. Write the ones digit, 3, in the ones column.	What is the tens digit in 19? __1__ Write 1 in the tens column. Write the ones digit, 9, in the ones column.	Add the ones. Regroup if you need to. Add the tens.

STEP 1

Tens	Ones
4	3
+	

STEP 2

Tens	Ones
4	3
+ 1	9

STEP 3

Tens	Ones
1	
4	3
+ 1	9
6	2

Rewrite the numbers. Then add.

1. $26 + 9$

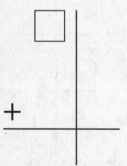

2. $16 + 43$

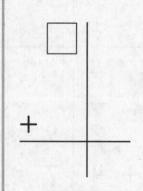

3. $32 + 38$

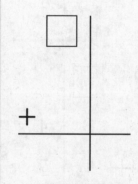

4. $23 + 26$

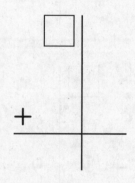

Problem Solving

Draw a Diagram • Addition

Hannah has 14 pencils. Juan has 13 pencils.
How many pencils do they have in all?

Unlock the Problem

What do I need to find?

~~how many pencils~~
_____

they have in all

**What information do
I need to use?**

Hannah has __14__ pencils.

Juan has __13__ pencils.

Show how to solve the problem.

Hannah's 14 pencils	Juan's 13 pencils

____ pencils in all

Hannah and Juan have __27__ pencils in all.

Solve.

1. There are 21 peanuts in a bag. 16 more
   peanuts are put into the bag. How many
   peanuts are in the bag in all?

21 peanuts	16 peanuts

_____ peanuts in all

_____ peanuts

Estimate Sums

When you estimate, you tell about how many.

$32 + 47 = $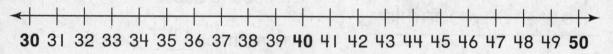

Is the sum greater or less than 100?
Find the closest ten for each addend.

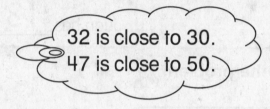

30 31 32 33 34 35 36 37 38 39 **40** 41 42 43 44 45 46 47 48 49 **50**

32 is close to 30.
47 is close to 50.

$30 + 50 = 80$

So, the sum of 32 and 47 is close to 80.
80 is <u>less than</u> 100.

Estimate the sum. Circle the better choice.

1. $32 + 39 = $ ▪

greater than 100

less than 100

2. $11 + 12 = $ ▪

greater than 50

less than 50

3. $46 + 30 = $ ▪

greater than 50

less than 50

4. $27 + 18 = $ ▪

greater than 20

less than 20

Find Sums for 3 Addends

You can add three numbers in different ways.
Start by adding the ones first.

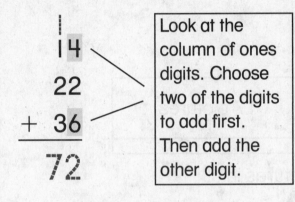

$$4 + 6 = 10$$
$$10 + 2 = 12$$

Then add the tens.

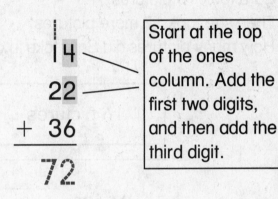

$$4 + 2 = 6$$
$$6 + 6 = 12$$

Then add the tens.

Add. Circle the numbers you will add first.

1.	2.	3.	4.
18	40	13	26
25	37	21	22
+ 32	+ 16	+ 34	+ 23

Represent Addition Problems

Use a bar model to show the problem.

Sara took 16 pictures.
Then she took 17 more pictures.
How many pictures did Sara take in all?

16 pictures	17 pictures

_____ pictures in all

Add to find the total.

$$\begin{array}{r} 16 \\ +\ 17 \\ \hline 33 \end{array}$$

So, the answer is __33__ pictures.

Complete the bar model.
Then solve the problem.

1. Josh has 18 basketball cards
   and 14 baseball cards. How many
   cards does he have in all?

_____ basketball cards	_____ baseball cards

_____ cards in all

_____ cards

Break Apart Ones to Subtract

$44 - 7 =$ _____ ?

Look at the ones digit in the first number. $\downarrow$ 44

Break apart ones in the next number
so that 4 is one of the addends.

$7 =$ __4__ $+$ __3__

Subtract those addends in two steps.
Use the number line to help you solve.

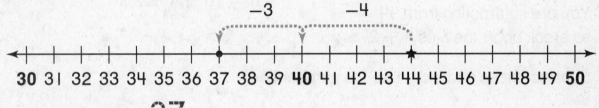

So, $44 - 7 =$ _37_.

Break apart ones to subtract. Write the difference.

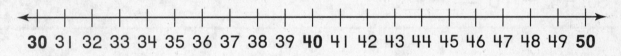

1. $42 - 8 =$ _____

2. $47 - 8 =$ _____

3. $46 - 9 =$ _____

4. $42 - 7 =$ _____

5. $43 - 5 =$ _____

6. $41 - 8 =$ _____

Break Apart Numbers to Subtract

$44 - 16 = $ ___?___

Break apart the number you are
subtracting into tens and ones.

$16 = $ __10__ $ + $ __6__

Then, break the single-digit addend apart.
One of the numbers should match
the ones digit of the number you
are subtracting from.

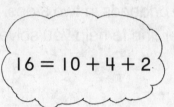

$16 = 10 + 4 + 2$

You are subtracting from 44,
so break apart the 6 as $4 + 2$.

Subtract these addends. Use the number line.

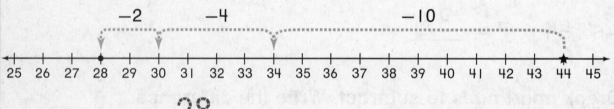

So, $44 - 16 = $ __28__ .

Break apart the number you are subtracting.
Write the difference.

```
 30 31 32 33 34 35 36 37 38 39 40 41 42 43 44 45 46 47 48 49 50 51 52 53 54 55 56 57 58 59 60
```

1. $51 - 16 = $ ____

2. $57 - 18 = $ ____

3. $55 - 17 = $ ____

4. $53 - 19 = $ ____

5. $54 - 17 = $ ____

6. $52 - 18 = $ ____

Model Regrouping for Subtraction

Subtract 37 from 65.

Are there enough ones to subtract 7? __no__
So, you will need to regroup.

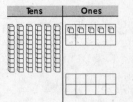

Trade 1 ten for
10 ones.

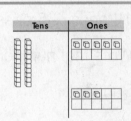

15 ones − 7 ones = ___8___ ones

5 tens − 3 tens = ___2___ tens

___2___ tens ___8___ ones is the same as ___28___.

The difference is ___28___.

Write how many tens and ones. Write the difference.

1. Subtract 4 from 41.

Tens	Ones

_____ tens _____ ones

_____

2. Subtract 18 from 43.

Tens	Ones

_____ tens _____ ones

_____

3. Subtract 19 from 55.

Tens	Ones

_____ tens _____ ones

_____

Model and Record 2-Digit Subtraction

Subtract.   54
           − 15

Look at the quick pictures. Are there
enough ones to subtract 5? __no__

Tens	Ones
5	4
− 1	5

Regroup 1 ten as 10 ones.

Write the new number
of tens and ones.

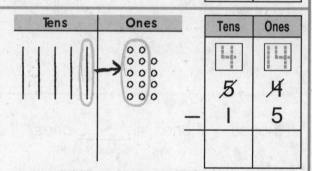

Tens	Ones
4	14
5̶	4̶
− 1	5

Subtract.

14 ones − 5 ones = __9__ ones

Write that number in the ones place.

Subtract.

4 tens − 1 ten = __3__ tens

Write that number in the tens place.

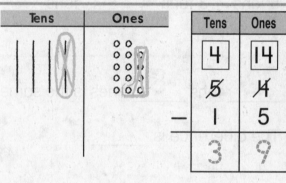

Tens	Ones
4	14
5̶	4̶
− 1	5
3	9

Draw a quick picture to solve. Write the difference.

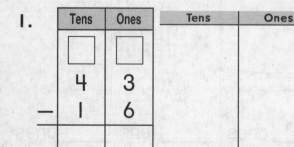

1.

Tens	Ones
4	3
− 1	6

Tens	Ones

2.

Tens	Ones
3	1
− 1	7

Tens	Ones

Name _____

2-Digit Subtraction

Subtract.   54
           − 28

Are there enough
ones to subtract 8? __no__

Tens	Ones
5	4
− 2	8

Regroup 1 ten as 10 ones.
Record the regrouping:
4 tens 14 ones

Tens	Ones
4	14
5	4
− 2	8

Subtract.
14 ones − 8 ones = __6__ ones

Write that number in the ones place.

Tens	Ones
4	14
5	4
− 2	8
	6

Subtract.
4 tens − 2 tens = __2__ tens

Write that number in the tens place.

Tens	Ones
4	14
5	4
− 2	8
2	6

Regroup if you need to. Write the difference.

1.

Tens	Ones
7	2
− 4	5

2.

Tens	Ones
5	1
− 1	3

3.

Tens	Ones
3	8
− 1	6

Practice 2-Digit Subtraction

Clay scored 80 points. Meg scored 61 points.
How many more points did Clay score than Meg?

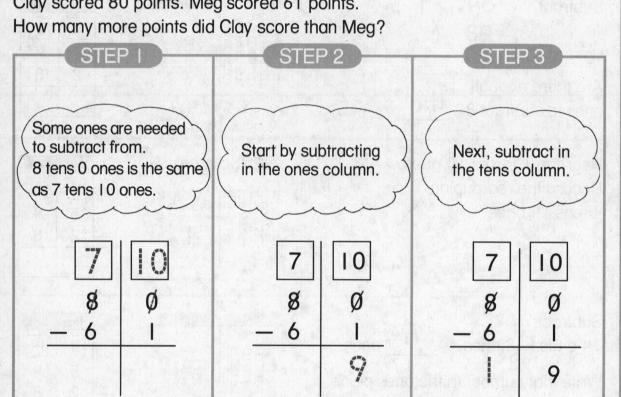

STEP 1	STEP 2	STEP 3

Some ones are needed to subtract from.
8 tens 0 ones is the same as 7 tens 10 ones.

Start by subtracting in the ones column.

Next, subtract in the tens column.

Write the difference.

1.
```
  6  4
- 2  7
```

2.
```
  3  7
- 2  2
```

3.
```
  6  1
- 4  8
```

4.
```
  7  4
- 2  6
```

5.
```
  3  7
- 1  9
```

6.
```
  5  5
- 1  4
```

Rewrite 2-Digit Subtraction

Subtract. $62 - 38 = ?$

Rewrite 62.

	62	

The 6 is in the tens place. Write it in the tens column.

The 2 is in the ones place. Write it in the ones column.

Tens	Ones
6	2
−	

Rewrite 38.

	38	

The 3 is in the tens place. Write it in the tens column.

The 8 is in the ones place. Write it in the ones column.

Tens	Ones
6	2
− 3	8

Now the ones digits are in a column and the tens digits are in a column.

Subtract. Write the difference.

Tens	Ones
5	12
6	2
− 3	8
2	4

Rewrite the numbers. Then subtract.

1. $56 - 24$

Tens	Ones
−	

2. $74 - 37$

Tens	Ones
−	

3. $43 - 15$

Tens	Ones
−	

Problem Solving

Draw a Diagram • Subtraction

Katie had a box of 46 craft sticks. She used 28 craft sticks to make a sailboat. How many craft sticks were not used?

Unlock the Problem

What do I need to find?	**What information do I need to use?**
how many craft sticks _____ were not used	Katie had 46 craft sticks . She used 28 craft sticks .

Show how to solve the problem.

28 craft sticks used	? craft sticks not used

46 craft sticks in all

_____ craft sticks were not used.

Solve.

1. Ms. Lee took 31 purses to the fair.
   She sold 17 purses. How many
   purses did she have left?

17 purses sold	? purses left

31 purses in all

Ms. Lee had _____ purses left.

Name _____

Represent Subtraction Problems

Use a bar model to show the problem.

37 birds were in the trees.

13 birds flew away.

How many birds are in the trees now?

13 birds	? birds

37 birds in all

Subtract to find the missing part.

So, the answer is __24__ birds.

$$\begin{array}{r} 37 \\ -13 \\ \hline 24 \end{array}$$

**Label the bar model to show the problem.
Then solve.**

1. Gina has 23 pens. 15 pens are blue
   and the rest are red. How many pens
   are red?

____ blue pens	____ red pens

____ pens in all

____ red pens

Solve Multistep Problems

Mr. Wright had 34 blue pencils and 25 red pencils. He gave 42 pencils to students. How many pencils does he have now?

The first sentence tells you what Mr. Wright had.

blue pencils

and

red pencils

$$\begin{array}{r} 34 \\ + 25 \\ \hline 59 \end{array}$$

The second sentence tells you that he gave 42 of the pencils to students.

pencils

$$\begin{array}{r} 59 \\ - 42 \\ \hline \end{array}$$

Mr. Wright has _____ pencils now.

Solve the problem in steps. Show what you did.

1. Kara had 37 stickers. She gave 11 stickers to Sam and 5 stickers to Jane. How many stickers does Kara have now?

_____ stickers

Take a Survey

You can take a survey to get information.

(Which is your favorite sport?)

Each tally mark stands for one person's answer.
The numbers show how many tally marks there are.

Favorite Sport		
Sport	**Tally**	**Total**
soccer	IIII	4
basketball	IIII I	5
football	III	3

Elijah asked his classmates to choose their favorite breakfast food. He makes this chart.

Favorite Breakfast Food		
Food	**Tally**	**Total**
cereal	IIII	4
pancakes	IIII III	
toast	III	
eggs	IIII	

1. Write numbers to complete the chart.

2. How many classmates chose pancakes?

_____ classmates

3. Which breakfast food did the fewest classmates choose?

_____

Problem Solving
Make a List • Surveys

Wendy took a survey of her classmates. She asked this question.

Which is your favorite ride at the amusement park the merry-go-round, the roller coaster, or the bumper cars?

Which ride did the most classmates choose?

merry-go-round	bumper cars
roller coaster	merry-go-round
bumper cars	bumper cars
bumper cars	roller coaster
merry-go-round	merry-go-round
bumper cars	roller coaster

Unlock the Problem

What do I need to find?

which _____ride_____ the most classmates chose

What information do I need to use?

_____number of votes_____ there are for each ride

Show how to solve the problem.

Complete the chart.

Favorite Ride at the Amusement Park		
Ride	**Tally**	**Total**
merry-go-round	IIII	4
roller coaster		
bumper cars		

The most classmates chose _____.

Name _____

Pictographs

A pictograph uses pictures to show information.
Look at the key to find what each picture stands for.

Animals at the Pet Store	
Animal	**Tally**
fish	IIIII III
hamster	IIII
turtle	IIIII I

Animals at the Pet Store					
fish	◆	◆	◆	◆	
hamster	◆	◆			
turtle	◆	◆	◆		

Key: Each ◆ stands for 2 animals.

How many turtles are there in the pet store? __6 turtles__

1. Use the tally chart to complete the pictograph.
   Draw a ☺ for every 2 children.

Favorite Color	
Color	**Tally**
pink	IIIII I
yellow	IIII
blue	IIIII III

Favorite Color				
pink	☺	☺	☺	
yellow				
blue				

Key: Each ☺ stands for 2 children.

2. Which color did the fewest children choose? _____

_____

3. How many children chose pink? _____ children

_____

4. Which color did the most children choose? _____

Make Bar Graphs

These bar graphs show how many games Alex, Sarah, and Tony played. Both graphs show the same data.

- Alex played 5 games.
- Sarah played 3 games.
- Tony played 4 games.

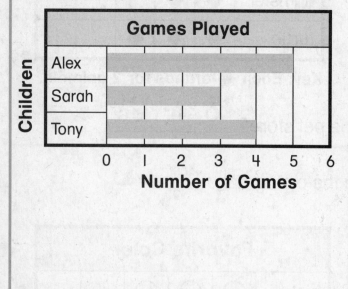

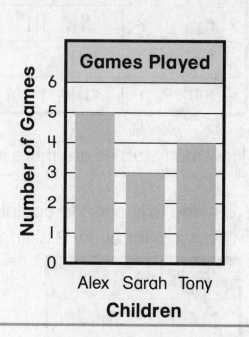

Jim is making a bar graph to show the number of markers his friends have.

- Adam has 4 markers.
- Clint has 3 markers.
- Erin has 2 markers.

1. Write labels for the graph.

_____

2. Draw bars to show the number of markers that Clint and Erin have.

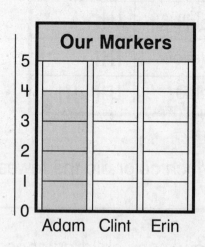

Name _____

Use Bar Graphs

Bar graphs can have different scales.

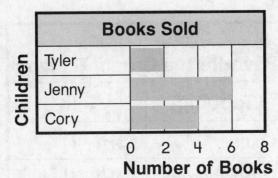

On this graph, the scale shows skip counting by twos.

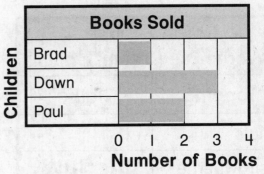

On this graph, the scale shows counting by ones.

Use the bar graph.

1. Which group has the fewest children?

   _____

2. How many children are in Group C?

   _____ children

3. In which group are there 12 children?

   _____

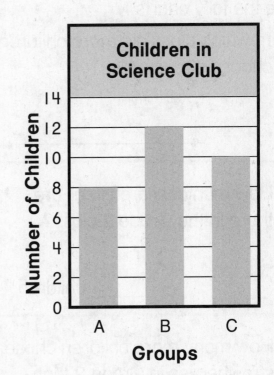

Use Data

These charts show information about favorite
ice-cream toppings for two classes.

Grade 2 Class Favorite Ice-Cream Topping	
Topping	Tally
nuts	II
strawberries	HHT IIII
peaches	HHT

Grade 4 Class Favorite Ice-Cream Topping	
Topping	Tally
nuts	HHT I
strawberries	HHT II
peaches	IIII

Use the tally charts.

1. In which class did more children choose strawberries?

_____

2. In which class did fewer children choose peaches?

_____

3. How many children in all are there in the Grade 2 class?

_____ children

4. How many children in all are there in the Grade 4 class?

_____ children

5. How many more children chose strawberries in Grade 2 than in Grade 4?

_____ more children

6. How many children in the Grade 2 class chose a topping other than peaches?

_____ children

Break Apart 3-Digit Addends

Use these steps to add.

$$749$$
$$+126$$

Step 1 Break apart each addend by the value of each digit.

$$749 = \underline{700} + \underline{40} + \underline{9}$$
$$+126 = \underline{100} + \underline{20} + \underline{6}$$

Step 2 Add the hundreds, tens, and ones.
Step 3 Add these sums together.

Hundreds	Tens	Ones

$$749 \quad \underline{700} + \underline{40} + \underline{9}$$
$$+126 \quad \underline{100} + \underline{20} + \underline{6}$$
$$\underline{800} + \underline{60} + \underline{15} = \underline{875}$$

Break apart the addends. Solve for the total sum.

Hundreds	Tens	Ones

1. $254 \longrightarrow \underline{} + \underline{} + \underline{}$

   $+536 \longrightarrow \underline{} + \underline{} + \underline{}$

   $\underline{} + \underline{} + \underline{} = \underline{}$

Record 3-Digit Addition: Regroup Ones

Add.   318
     + 257

Hundreds	Tens	Ones
3	[1]	8
+ 2	5	7

Add the ones.

$8 + 7 = \underline{15}$

Do you need to regroup? __yes__

Regroup 10 ones as 1 ten.

Hundreds	Tens	Ones
3	[1]	8
+ 2	5	7
		5

Add the tens.

$1 + 1 + 5 = \underline{7}$

Add the hundreds.

$3 + 2 = \underline{5}$

Hundreds	Tens	Ones
3	[1]	8
+ 2	5	7
5	7	5

Write the sum.

1.

Hundreds	Tens	Ones
	[ ]	
4	5	7
+ 3	3	5

2.

Hundreds	Tens	Ones
	[ ]	
5	2	6
+ 1	4	2

3.

Hundreds	Tens	Ones
	[ ]	
7	3	3
+ 2	2	9

© Houghton Mifflin Harcourt Publishing Company

Name _____

Record 3-Digit Addition: Regroup Tens

Add. 271
     + 158

Add the ones.

1 + 8 = ___9___

Hundreds	Tens	Ones
		1
2	7	1
+ 1	5	8
		9

Add the **tens.**

7 + 5 = ___12___

Do you need to regroup? ___yes___

Regroup 10 tens as 1 hundred.

Hundreds	Tens	Ones
1		
2	7	1
+ 1	5	8
	2	9

Add the hundreds.

1 + 2 + 1 = ___4___

Hundreds	Tens	Ones
1		
2	7	1
+ 1	5	8
4	2	9

Write the sum.

1.

Hundreds	Tens	Ones
2	6	4
+ 1	4	5

2.

Hundreds	Tens	Ones
1	5	3
+ 5	9	2

3.

Hundreds	Tens	Ones
2	3	2
+ 6	0	6

3-Digit Addition

Use these steps to regroup more than once.

189
+ 623

Step 1 Add the ones. If the sum is
10 or greater, regroup.

9 ones + 3 ones = 12 ones

12 ones = 1 ten 2 ones

Step 2 Add the tens. Regroup if needed.

1 ten + 8 tens + 2 tens = 11 tens

11 tens = 1 hundred 1 ten

Step 3 Add the hundreds.

1 hundred + 1 hundred + 6 hundreds = 8 hundreds

```
  1   8   9
+ 6   2   3
  8   1   2
```

Write the sum.

1.
```
  2   7   8
+ 4   6   5
```

2.
```
  3   7   7
+ 2   4   3
```

3.
```
  4   6   5
+ 3   1   2
```

4.
```
  1   5   7
+ 7   7   1
```

5.
```
  2   5   5
+ 3   6   8
```

6.
```
  3   6   4
+ 4   1   9
```

Name _____

Practice 3-Digit Addition

Louis has 135 bear stamps and 167 duck stamps.
How many stamps does he have?

Add the ones. Regroup 10 ones as 1 ten.	Add the tens. Regroup 10 tens as 1 hundred.	Add the hundreds.
$\begin{array}{r} 1 \\ 1\ 3\ 5 \\ +\ 1\ 6\ 7 \\ \hline 2 \end{array}$	$\begin{array}{r} 1\ 1 \\ 1\ 3\ 5 \\ +\ 1\ 6\ 7 \\ \hline 0\ 2 \end{array}$	$\begin{array}{r} 1\ 1 \\ 1\ 3\ 5 \\ +\ 1\ 6\ 7 \\ \hline 3\ 0\ 2 \end{array}$

There are 0 tens after regrouping.
Use 0 as a place holder.

Louis has __302__ stamps.

Add.

1.
$\begin{array}{r} 1 \\ 3\ 4\ 5 \\ +\ 1\ 8\ 3 \\ \hline 5\ 2\ 8 \end{array}$

2.
$\begin{array}{r} 6\ 8\ 7 \\ +\ \ \ 2\ 6 \\ \hline \end{array}$

3.
$\begin{array}{r} 2\ 9\ 1 \\ +\ 4\ 2\ 7 \\ \hline \end{array}$

4.
$\begin{array}{r} 5\ 2\ 6 \\ +\ \ \ 5\ 7 \\ \hline \end{array}$

5.
$\begin{array}{r} 4\ 3\ 8 \\ +\ 3\ 7\ 1 \\ \hline \end{array}$

6.
$\begin{array}{r} 6\ 5\ 6 \\ +\ 2\ 1\ 3 \\ \hline \end{array}$

7.
$\begin{array}{r} 1\ 7\ 8 \\ +\ 1\ 1\ 9 \\ \hline \end{array}$

8.
$\begin{array}{r} 4\ 6\ 2 \\ +\ 5\ 2\ 3 \\ \hline \end{array}$

9.
$\begin{array}{r} 5\ 8\ 2 \\ +\ \ \ 3\ 6 \\ \hline \end{array}$

Problem Solving

Make a Model • 3-Digit Subtraction

There were 237 books on the shelves. Mr. Davies took 126 off the shelves. How many books were still on the shelves?

Unlock the Problem

What do I need to find?	**What information do I need to use?**
how many books were still on the shelves.	There were __237__ books on the shelves. Mr. Davies took __126__ books off the shelves.

Show how to solve the problem.

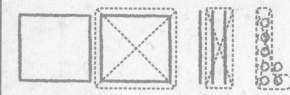

There were _____ books still on the shelves.

Make a model.
Show how you solved the problem.

1. Mr. Cho drove 256 miles on Monday.
   On Tuesday he drove 132 miles.
   How many more miles did he
   drive on Monday than on Tuesday?

_____ more miles

Name _____

Record 3-Digit Subtraction: Regroup Tens

Subtract. 463
-317

Are there enough ones to subtract 7? __no__
Regroup 1 ten as 10 ones.

Hundreds	Tens	Ones
4	6	3
3	1	7

Now there are __13__ ones and __5__ tens.
Subtract the ones.
$13 - 7 = $ __6__

Hundreds	Tens	Ones
	5	13
4	6	3
3	1	7
		6

Subtract the tens.
$5 - 1 = $ __4__
Subtract the hundreds.
$4 - 3 = $ __1__

Hundreds	Tens	Ones
	5	13
4	6	3
3	1	7
1	4	6

Solve. Write the difference.

1.

Hundreds	Tens	Ones
8	6	2
3	2	8

2.

Hundreds	Tens	Ones
6	7	8
2	4	5

3.

Hundreds	Tens	Ones
4	7	6
1	4	8

Record 3-Digit Subtraction: Regroup Hundreds

Subtract.   326
           − 174

Subtract the ones.

$6 - 4 = \underline{2}$

Are there enough tens to subtract 7 tens? ___no___

Hundreds	Tens	Ones
2	12	
3	2	6
− 1	7	4
		2

Regroup 1 hundred as 10 tens.

- -

Now there are __12__ tens

and __2__ hundreds.

Subtract the tens.

$12 - 7 = \underline{5}$

Subtract the hundreds.

$2 - 1 = \underline{1}$

Hundreds	Tens	Ones
2	12	
3	2	6
− 1	7	4
1	5	2

Solve. Write the difference.

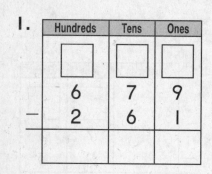

1.

Hundreds	Tens	Ones
6	7	9
− 2	6	1

2.

Hundreds	Tens	Ones
5	2	5
− 2	9	3

3.

Hundreds	Tens	Ones
8	5	9
− 4	7	2

Name _____

Skip Count on a Hundred Chart

Look at the shaded numbers on the hundred chart.

This pattern shows
skip counting by tens.
What number comes next
in the pattern after 60?

Think:
The shaded
numbers have a 0
in the ones place.

Skip count by tens to
continue the pattern.
Shade the squares.

1	2	3	4	5	6	7	8	9	10
11	12	13	14	15	16	17	18	19	20
21	22	23	24	25	26	27	28	29	30
31	32	33	34	35	36	37	38	39	40
41	42	43	44	45	46	47	48	49	50
51	52	53	54	55	56	57	58	59	60
61	62	63	64	65	66	67	68	69	70
71	72	73	74	75	76	77	78	79	80
81	82	83	84	85	86	87	88	89	90
91	92	93	94	95	96	97	98	99	100

Skip count. Show the pattern on the hundred chart.

1. Count by twos.
   Shade the squares.

2. Count by fives.
   Circle the numbers.

3. Write the beginning of
   the pattern made with
   the circled numbers.

1	2	3	4	5	6	7	8	9	10
11	12	13	14	15	16	17	18	19	20
21	22	23	24	25	26	27	28	29	30
31	32	33	34	35	36	37	38	39	40
41	42	43	44	45	46	47	48	49	50
51	52	53	54	55	56	57	58	59	60
61	62	63	64	65	66	67	68	69	70
71	72	73	74	75	76	77	78	79	80
81	82	83	84	85	86	87	88	89	90
91	92	93	94	95	96	97	98	99	100

5, 10, _____, _____, _____, _____, _____, _____, _____, 50

Problem Solving
Act It Out • Patterns

Clarence puts 5 grapes on each plate.
How many grapes in all does he put on 4 plates?

Unlock the Problem

What do I need to find?	**What information do I need to use?**
how many grapes he puts on the 4 plates	Clarence puts _____ grapes on each plate. He has _____ plates.

Show how to solve the problem.

Clarence puts _____ grapes on 4 plates.

Act it out. Draw. Then solve.

1. Rachel needs to put markers on 3 tables.
   Each table should have 6 markers.
   How many markers does she need in all?

Rachel needs _____ markers.

Algebra: Extend Patterns

How many wheels are on 5 scooters?

What do you need to find?

how many wheels are on 5 scooters

scooter

How would you solve this problem?

Use a pattern.

> There are 2 wheels on each scooter. The pattern is count by twos.

Continue the pattern. Complete the table.

number of scooters	1	2	3	4	5
number of wheels	2	4	6		

There are _____ wheels on 5 scooters.

Use the pattern. Complete the table to solve.

1. How many sails are on 5 boats?

> There are 5 sails on each boat.

number of boats	1	2	3	4	5
number of sails	5	10			

There are _____ sails on 5 boats.

Connect Addition and Multiplication

2 groups of 5

There are 2 trains. Each train has 5 cubes.
Add to find how many cubes in all.

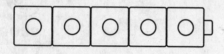

$$\begin{array}{r} 5 \\ +\ 5 \\ \hline 10 \end{array}$$

Multiply to find how many cubes in all.

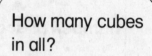

How many trains?   How many cubes in each train?   How many cubes in all?

_____ × _____ = _____

Show the addition.
Then write the multiplication sentence.

1. 2 groups of 3

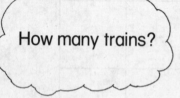

$$\begin{array}{r} 3 \\ +\ 3 \\ \hline \end{array}$$

_____

2. 2 groups of 4

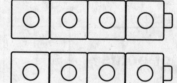

$$\begin{array}{r} 4 \\ +\ 4 \\ \hline \end{array}$$

_____

Model Multiplication

You can use squares on a grid to model multiplication.

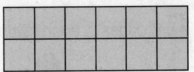

__2__ rows of __6__

__12__ in all

Write how many rows and how many in each row.
Write how many in all.

1. _____ rows of _____ _____ in all	2. _____ rows of _____ _____ in all
3. 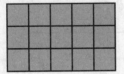 _____ rows of _____ _____ in all	4. _____ rows of _____ _____ in all
5.  _____ rows of _____ _____ in all	6. 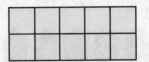 _____ rows of _____ _____ in all

Multiply with 2

There are 2 cubes in each tower.

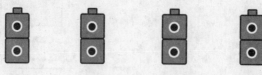

Skip count by twos. $\underline{2}$, $\underline{4}$, $\underline{6}$, $\underline{8}$

$$\underline{4 \times 2 = 8}$$

Skip count by twos.
Write the multiplication sentence.

1. $\underline{2 \times 2 =}$

2. _____

3. _____

4. _____

5. _____

6. _____

Name _____

Multiply with 5

There are 5 counters in each stack.

Skip count by fives.

5 , 10 , 15 , 20

4 × 5 = 20

Skip count by fives.
Write the multiplication sentence.

1.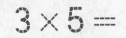

   3 × 5 =

2.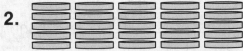

3.

   _____

4.

   _____

5.

   _____

6.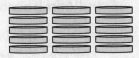

   _____

Indirect Measurement

You can compare the lengths of objects that are not near each other.

Cut a piece of string to match the length of one of the objects.
Compare the length of the string to the length of the other object.

The string that matches the length of the map is longer
than the door.

So, the map is _____longer_____ than the door.

Find the real objects. Use string and scissors.
Circle the picture that answers the question.

1. Which is shorter?

chair

lunch box

2. Which is longer?

book case

bulletin board

   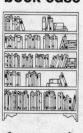

Compare Lengths

If a new string is longer than string B, how does string A compare to the new string?

A ▭

B ▭

C ┣- -

First, look at string A and string B.

Which string is shorter? ___A___

If string A is shorter than string B, a string that is longer than string B will also be longer than string A.

String A is ___shorter than___ the new string.

Write **shorter than** or **longer than**.

1. If a new string is shorter than string B, how does string A compare to the new string?

   A ▭

   B ▭

   String A is _____ the new string.

2. If a new string is longer than string B, how does string A compare to the new string?

   A ▭

   B ▭

   String A is _____ the new string.

Name _____

Measure with Inch Models

Each color tile is about 1 inch long.

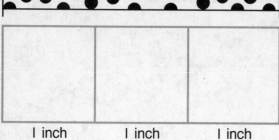

| 1 inch | 1 inch | 1 inch |

Think:
If 1 color tile
is 1 inch long,
then 2 color tiles
are 2 inches long.

Count the inches.

The ribbon is _____3_____ inches long.

Use color tiles. Measure the length of the object in inches.

1.

_____ inches

2.

_____ inches

3.

_____ inches

Make and Use a Ruler

Use a color tile to make a ruler on a paper strip.
Color the parts that are each about 1 inch long.

Your ruler is divided into ___ **1 inch** ___ sections.

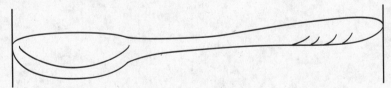

Line up the left edge of the bracelet with
the first mark. Count the inches.

The bracelet is __5__ inches long.

Measure the length with your ruler.
Count the inches.

1.

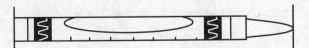

_____ inches

2.

_____ inches

Estimate Lengths

The bead is 1 inch long. Use this bead to estimate
how many beads will fit on the string.

Four beads will fit on the string.

So, the string is about __4__ inches long.

Circle the best estimate for the length of the string.

1.

2 inches   4 inches   6 inches

2.

1 inch   3 inches   5 inches

3.

1 inch   2 inches   4 inches

4.

5 inches   8 inches   10 inches

Name _____

Measure with an Inch Ruler

To measure, first line up the end of the object with
the zero mark on the ruler. Then find the inch mark
that is closest to the other end.

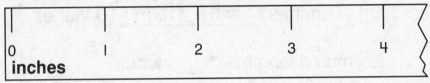

The length of the ribbon is ___3___ inches to the nearest inch.

Measure the length to the nearest inch.

1.

_____ inches

2.

_____ inch

3.

_____ inches

4.

_____ inches

Estimate and Measure Length

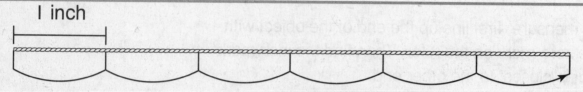

1 inch

Use the 1-inch mark to estimate. Is the string....

• more than or less than 4 inches? **more than** 4 inches

• more than or less than 10 inches? **less than** 10 inches

Estimated length: _____ inches

Use a ruler to measure.

Line up the zero mark on the ruler with the left side of the string. What inch mark is closest to the right side of the string?

Actual length: _____ inches

Estimate the length. Then measure with a ruler.

1.   1 inch

Estimated length: _____ inches

Actual length: _____ inches

2.   1 inch

Estimated length: _____ inches

Actual length: _____ inches

3.   1 inch

Estimated length: _____ inches

Actual length: _____ inches

Measure in Inches and Feet

12 inches is the same as 1 foot.

A folder is about 12 inches wide.
A folder is also about 1 foot wide.

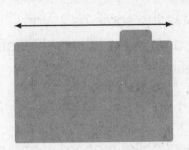

Measure to the nearest inch.
Then measure to the nearest foot.

Find the real object.	Measure.
1. desk	_____ inches _____ feet
2. bookshelf	_____ inches _____ feet
3. rug	_____ inches _____ feet
4. map	_____ inches _____ feet

Measure in Feet and Yards

3 feet is the same as 1 yard.
You can measure longer lengths
in feet and also in yards.

bulletin board

The real bulletin board is about 3 feet tall.
The real bulletin board is about 1 yard tall.

Measure to the nearest foot.
Then measure to the nearest yard.

Find the real object.	Measure.
1. **chalkboard** ![123 ABC]	_____ feet _____ yards
2. **window**	_____ feet _____ yards

Name _____

Measure with a Centimeter Model

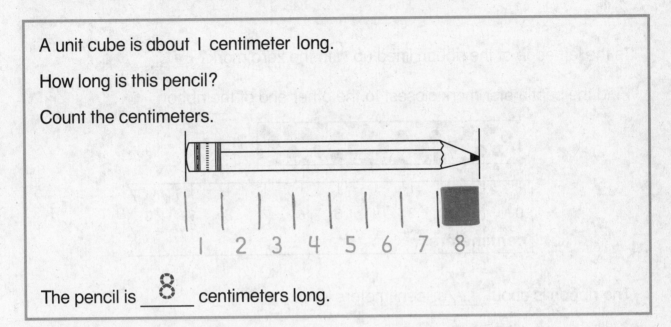

A unit cube is about 1 centimeter long.

How long is this pencil?

Count the centimeters.

1 2 3 4 5 6 7 8

The pencil is __8__ centimeters long.

Use a unit cube. Measure the length in centimeters.

1.

_____ centimeters

2.

_____ centimeters

3.

_____ centimeters

© Houghton Mifflin Harcourt Publishing Company

Measure with a Centimeter Ruler

Is the left edge of the ribbon lined up with the zero mark? **yes**

Find the centimeter mark closest to the other end of the ribbon.

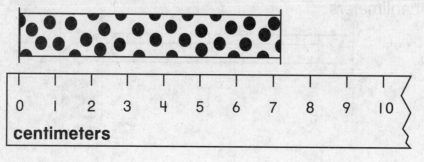

The ribbon is about __7__ centimeters long.

Measure the length to the nearest centimeter.

1.

_____ centimeters

2.

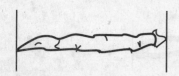

_____ centimeters

3.

_____ centimeters

Make Reasonable Estimates

The ribbon is about 8 centimeters long. Which is the
most reasonable estimate for the length of the string?

ribbon

2 centimeters

(6 centimeters)

10 centimeters

string

The ribbon is not
4 times as long as the
string. 2 centimeters
is not reasonable.

The string is shorter
than the ribbon.
10 centimeters is not
reasonable.

1. The rope is about 7 centimeters long. Circle the
best estimate for the length of the yarn.

rope

yarn

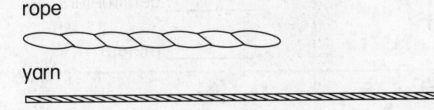

5 centimeters   9 centimeters   14 centimeters

2. The pencil is about 10 centimeters long. Circle the
best estimate for the length of the ribbon.

5 centimeters   9 centimeters   12 centimeters

Centimeters and Meters

You can measure longer
lengths in meters.

I meter is the same as
I00 centimeters.

The real board is about I00 centimeters tall.
The real board is also about I meter tall.

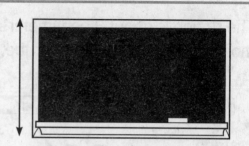

Measure to the nearest centimeter.
Then measure to the nearest meter.

Find the real object.	Measure.
1. desk	_____ centimeters _____ meters
2. door	_____ centimeters _____ meters
3. classroom floor	_____ centimeters _____ meters

Name _____

Problem Solving

Act It Out • Length

Brooke wants to measure the distance around
a wall clock in inches. She has an inch ruler,
a meterstick, and a piece of string. Which tools
should she use?

Unlock the Problem

What do I need to find?

what tools Brooke should
use to measure around
a clock

**What information do
I need to use?**

Brooke has _an inch ruler,_
a meterstick, and
a piece of string.

Show how to solve the problem.

Brooke can measure around the
clock with string. Then she can
measure the string with the inch
ruler.

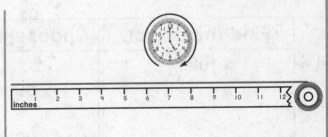

**Choose the better measurement tool.
Explain your choice.**

1. Jade wants to measure a library book. Which tool
should she use, an inch ruler or a yardstick?

Jade should use _____ because

_____

_____

Ounces and Pounds

Weight can be used to tell how heavy something is.

You can measure weight using ounces and pounds.

A paintbrush weighs

about __I ounce__.

> Use ounces to measure lighter objects.

A group of 16 paintbrushes

weighs about __I pound__.

> Use pounds to measure heavier objects.

There are 16 ounces in 1 pound.

Find the object.	Choose the unit.	Measure.
1. ruler	(ounce) pound	about _____ _____
2. tub of chalk	ounce pound	about _____ _____
3. marker	ounce pound	about _____ _____

Grams and Kilograms

Use grams and kilograms to measure mass.

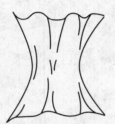

The mass of a tissue is

about __I gram__ .

The mass of a stack of paper

is about __I kilogram__ .

Use __grams__ to measure the mass of light objects.

Use __kilograms__ to measure the mass of heavy objects.

Find the object.	Choose the unit.	Measure.
1. **measuring tape**	(gram) kilogram	about _____
2. **group of blocks**	gram kilogram	about _____
3. **juice box**	gram kilogram	about _____

Cups and Quarts

You can measure the amount that a container can hold in cups or in quarts.

4 cups = 1 quart

1 cup

1 quart

<u>Cups</u> can be used to measure how much small containers hold.

<u>Quarts</u> can be used to measure how much larger containers hold.

Find the container.	Choose the unit.	Measure.
jar 1.	cup quart	about ____ _____
plastic bin 2.	cup quart	about ____ _____
bowl 3.	cup quart	about ____ _____

Milliliters and Liters

You can use milliliters and liters to measure capacity.

One milliliter is about 20 drops of water.

1,000 milliliters = 1 liter

1 __milliliter__ of water can fit
in a small spoon.

1 __liter__ of water can fit in a bucket.

Find the container.	Choose the unit.	Measure.
1. **juice box**	milliliter liter	about ____ _____
2. **milk jug**	milliliter liter	about ____ _____
3. **juice glass**	milliliter liter	about ____ _____

Choose the Unit

The size of an object or container can help you choose
the best unit to use to measure it.

When an object is light or a container
is small, use small units.

gram   milliliter

When an object is heavy or a container
is big, use larger units.

pound   quart

Circle the better unit of measure for the weight or
the mass of the object.

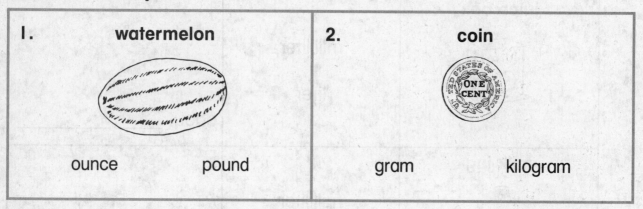

1.   **watermelon**

ounce   pound

2.   **coin**

gram   kilogram

Circle the better unit of measure for the capacity
of the container.

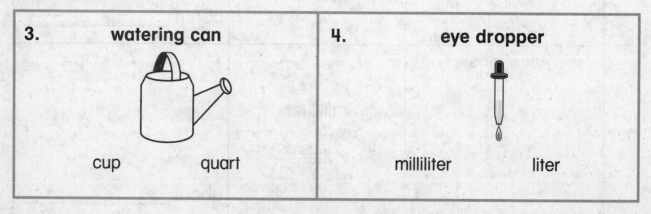

3.   **watering can**

cup   quart

4.   **eye dropper**

milliliter   liter

Name _____

Problem Solving

Act It Out • Measurement

Brett wants to find out how long a piece of string is.
He has these tools. Which measuring tool should he use?

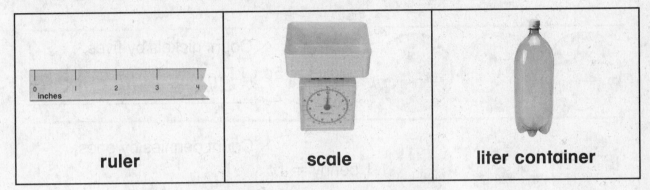

| ruler | scale | liter container |

Unlock the Problem

What do I need to find?

which _measuring tool_
Brett should use to find how long
the string is

What information do I need to use?

Brett has _a ruler, a scale,_
and a liter container.

Show how to solve the problem.

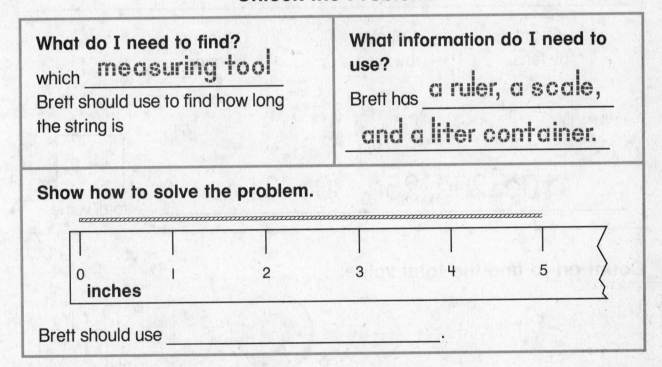

Brett should use _____.

Choose the best tool. Explain your choice.

1. Carey wants to find out how much her shoe weighs.
   Which tool should she use?

   Carey should use _____ because

   _____

Dimes, Nickels, and Pennies

I dime = 10¢

Count dimes by tens.

10¢, 20¢, 30¢

I nickel = 5¢

Count nickels by fives.

5¢, 10¢, 15¢

I penny = 1¢

Count pennies by ones.

1¢, 2¢, 3¢

Count by tens.

Count on by fives.

Count on by ones.

10¢, 20¢, 25¢, 30¢, 31¢

31¢

total value

Count on to find the total value.

1.

_____

total value

2.

_____

total value

Half Dollars and Quarters

I quarter = 25¢

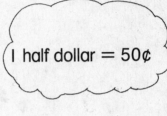 I half dollar = 50¢

50¢, 75¢, 85¢, 95¢, 96¢

96¢
total value

Count on to find the total value.

1.

_____ □ total value

2.

_____ □ total value

Count Collections

Draw the coins. Order them by value. Start
with the coin that has the greatest value.

50¢ 25¢ 5¢ I¢

Start at 50¢. Count on.

50¢, 75¢, 80¢, 8I¢
_____

The total value is __81¢__.

Draw and label the coins from greatest to least value. Find the total value.

I.    _____

_____

2.    _____

_____

3.    _____

Problem Solving
Find a Pattern • Money

Al has 3 dimes. He wants to trade them for nickels.
How many nickels should he get?

Unlock the Problem

What do I need to find?

how many nickels

Al should get

What information do I need to use?

Al has __3__ dimes.

I dime equals __2__ nickels.

Show how to solve the problem.
Use a pattern to complete the table.

dimes	1	2	3
nickels	2	4	6

Al should get __6__ nickels.

Find a pattern. Complete the table.

1. Ella has 4 dimes. She wants to trade them for
pennies. How many pennies should she get?

> I dime has the same value as 10 pennies.

dimes	1	2	3	4
pennies				

Ella should get _____ pennies.

One Dollar

One dollar has the same value as 100 cents.

$1.00 = 100¢

When you write $1.00, you use a dollar sign and a decimal point.

Count on to 100¢ to show $1.00.

25¢, 50¢, 75¢, 100¢ $1.00

total value

Draw the coins to show $1.00.
Write the total value.

1. dimes

_____

2. nickels

Name _____

Telling Time

When the hour hand points to a number, it is a time to the hour.

The hour hand is pointing to the 12.

The time is ___12:00___ .

When the hour hand is pointing halfway between numbers, it is half past an hour.

The hour hand is pointing halfway between the 12 and the 1.

The time is ___half past 12:00___ .

Look at where the hour hand points.
Write the time.

1.

_____

2.

_____

3.

_____

4.

_____

Time to the Hour and Half Hour

What time does each clock show?

The minute hand points to the
12 when it is time to the hour.

The minute hand points to the
6 when it is half past the hour.

Look at the clock hands.
Write the time.

1.

2.

3.

4.

5.

6.

Time to 5 Minutes

The minute hand moves from one number to the next in 5 minutes.

Start at the I2. Skip count by fives.

Stop at the number the minute hand points to.

The hour is 8 o'clock.

It is 20 minutes after 8:00.

Look at the clock hands.
Write the time.

I.

2.

3.

4.

5.

6.

Reteach
© Houghton Mifflin Harcourt Publishing Company

Grade 2

Time to the Minute

Each mark on the clock shows 1 minute.

Start at the 12. Skip count by fives
and then count on by ones.

Stop at the mark that the minute
hand points to.

The hour is 5 o'clock. It is 13 minutes
after 5:00.

Look at the clock hands.
Write the time.

1.

:

2.

:

3.

:

4.

:

5.

:

6.

:

Name _____

Units of Time

Look at how units of time are related. Then compare different amounts of time.

7 days is the same as 1 week.

10 days is _more than_ 1 week.

6 days is _less than_ 1 week.

Time Relationships
There are 60 minutes in 1 hour.
There are 24 hours in 1 day.
There are 7 days in 1 week.
There are about 4 weeks in 1 month.
There are 12 months in 1 year.

Write **more than** or **less than** to complete the sentence.

1. Kate kept her library book for 24 days.

   7 days is the same as 1 week.

   24 days is _____ 1 week.

2. The skating rink was closed for 6 months.

   12 months is the same as 1 year.

   6 months is _____ 1 year.

3. John studied for 45 minutes.

   60 minutes is the same as 1 hour.

   45 minutes is _____ 1 hour.

4. Rex was at baseball camp for 8 days.

   7 days is the same as 1 week.

   8 days is _____ 1 week.

Three-Dimensional Shapes

Look at the shapes of these three-dimensional objects.

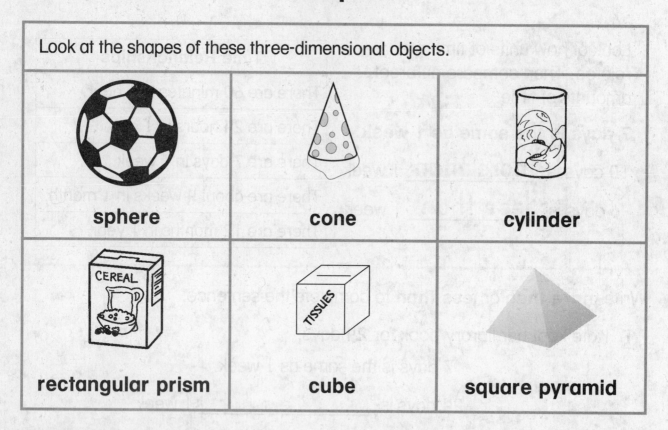

sphere	cone	cylinder
rectangular prism	cube	square pyramid

Circle the objects that match the shape name.

1. rectangular prism			
2. cylinder			
3. cone			

Two-Dimensional Shapes

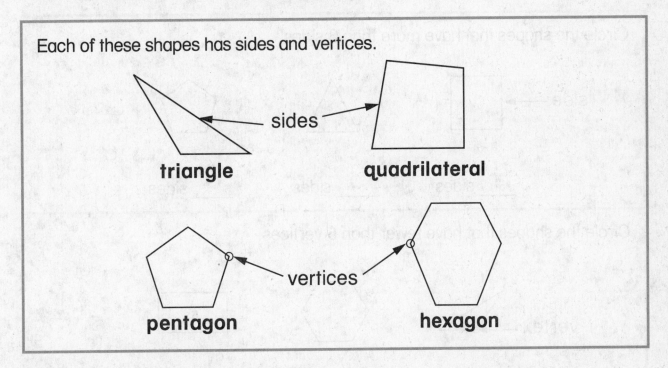

Each of these shapes has sides and vertices.

sides

triangle

quadrilateral

vertices

pentagon

hexagon

**Use a crayon to trace each side. Circle each vertex.
Write the number of sides and vertices.**

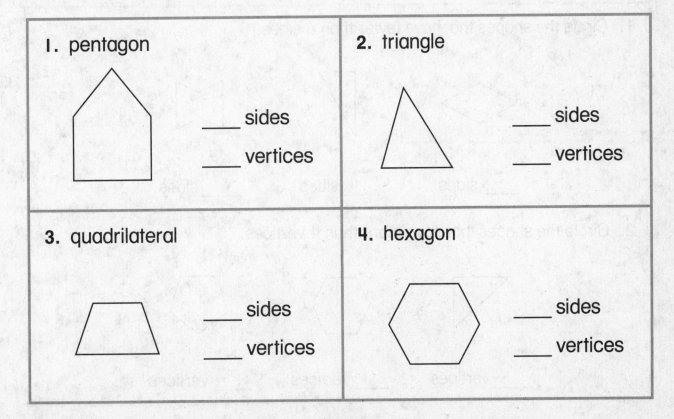

I. pentagon

____ sides

____ vertices

2. triangle

____ sides

____ vertices

3. quadrilateral

____ sides

____ vertices

4. hexagon

____ sides

____ vertices

Sort Two-Dimensional Shapes

Circle the shapes that have more than 3 sides.

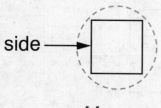 

_4_ sides   _3_ sides   _5_ sides

Circle the shapes that have fewer than 5 vertices.

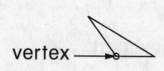

_3_ vertices   ___ vertices   ___ vertices

1. Circle the shapes that have fewer than 6 sides.

___ sides   ___ sides   ___ sides

2. Circle the shapes that have more than 4 vertices.

___ vertices   ___ vertices   ___ vertices

Symmetry

When you fold these shapes on the dashed line, the two parts match.

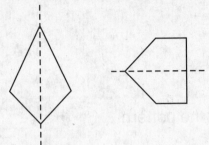

The dashed line is a line of symmetry.

These shapes do not have a line of symmetry.

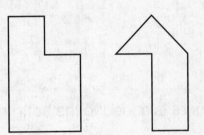

Is the dashed line a line of symmetry?

Circle yes or no.

1.

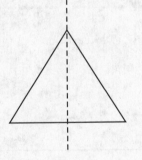

yes   no

2.

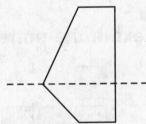

yes   no

3.

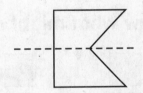

yes   no

4.

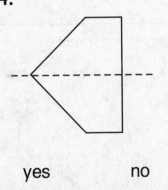

yes   no

5.

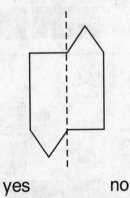

yes   no

6.

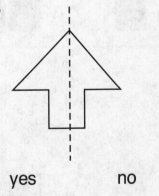

yes   no

Name _____

Algebra: Extend Growing Patterns

Look closely. How does the pattern grow?

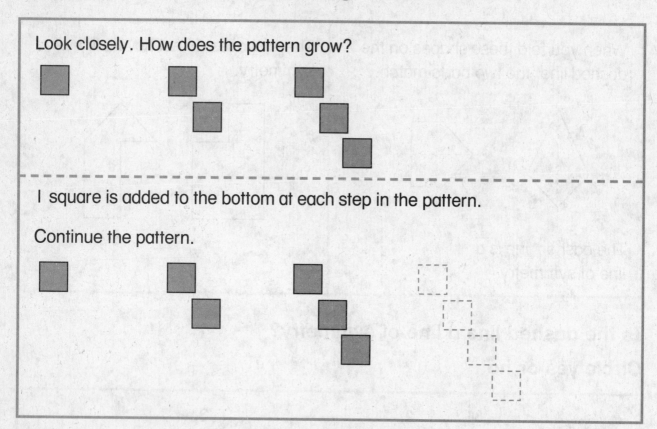

1 square is added to the bottom at each step in the pattern.

Continue the pattern.

Draw what might come next in the pattern.

1.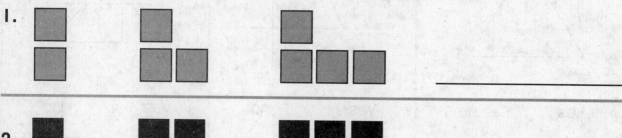

_____

2.

_____

3.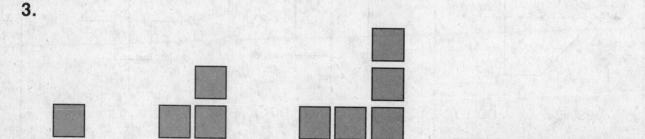

_____

Name _____

Problem Solving

Find a Pattern • Number Patterns

Emily made a pattern with 2 pennies in the first row,
5 pennies in the second row, and 8 pennies in the
third row. How many pennies should she put in the
sixth row?

Unlock the Problem

What do I need to find?	**What information do I need to use?**
how many pennies are in the 6th row	2 pennies in first row, 5 pennies in second row, 8 pennies in third row

Show how to solve the problem.

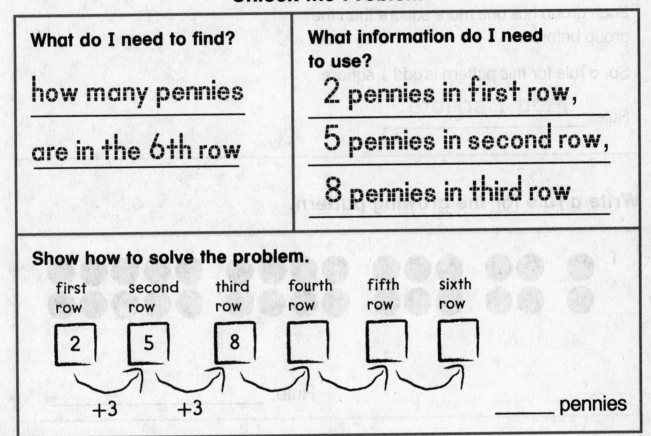

_____ pennies

Solve. Draw to show what you did.

1. Matthew made a pattern with 5 cars in the first row,
   10 cars in the second row, and 15 cars in the third
   row. How many cars should he put in the sixth row?

_____ cars

Name _____

Algebra: Find a Rule • Growing Patterns

This growing pattern is made with squares.

How do the groups of squares change?

Each group has one more square than the group before it.

So, a rule for this pattern is add 1 square.

Rule: ___Add 1 square.___

Write a rule for the growing pattern.

1.

Rule: _____

2.

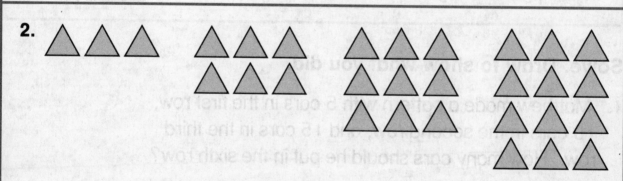

Rule: _____

Algebra: Explain Rules for Patterns

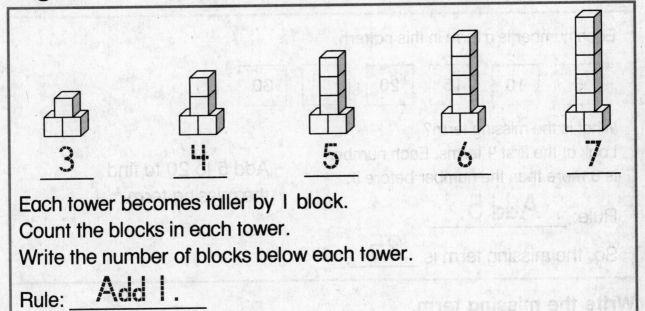

Each tower becomes taller by 1 block.
Count the blocks in each tower.
Write the number of blocks below each tower.

Rule: _____Add 1._____

Write the number of squares in each step.
Write a rule for the growing pattern.

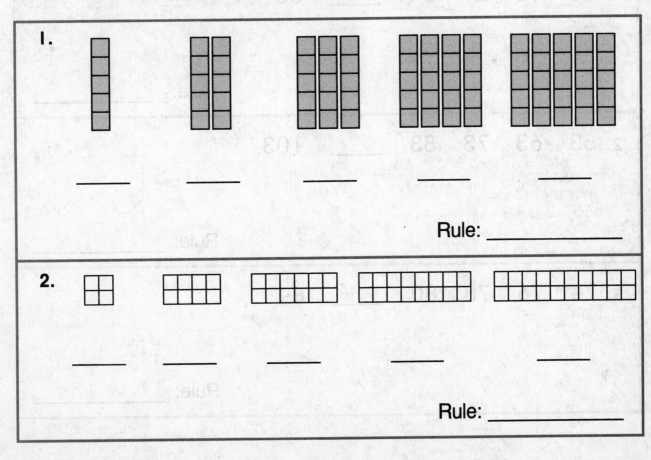

1.

_____   _____   _____   _____   _____

Rule: _____

2.

_____   _____   _____   _____   _____

Rule: _____

Algebra: Find Missing Terms for Patterns

Each number is a term in this pattern.

5	10	15	20		30

What is the missing term?
Look at the first 4 terms. Each number
is 5 more than the number before it.

Add 5 to 20 to find
the missing term.

Rule: ___*Add 5.*___

So, the missing term is ___25___.

Write the missing term.
Then write a rule.

1. 15   18   21   24   ____   30

   Rule: _____

2. 53   63   73   83   ____   103

   Rule: _____

3. 74   76   78   80   ____   84

   Rule: _____